Think Like A Caveman

...remembering the organic life.

A *My Mind and Me* Publication

Written by Jeff Lethcoe
Illustrated by Jason Lethcoe
Copyright 2010

For my wife, Elaine.
Thank you for choosing your adventure with me.

Introduction

Carl spent a good many hours lying with his naked back pressed against the cool, damp soil. He had hewn out a cave at the bottom of the tallest mountain as his stake, and he couldn't be happier with his decision. The dank, earthy air and the moist, loose dirt made him feel one with nature- a part of it, like a root coming out of the ground. He rolled and sniffed as a lazy smile gently spread over his rocky teeth. Besides eating, Carl loved nothing more than to bury himself under mounds of freshly dug earth, close his eyes and think. He was a man, and it was a man's privilege to be a thinker; Carl knew it and so did all of the others. He relished this thought often, and as a reward, he afforded himself frequent naps inside the home he had made with his own hands.

    Every now and again, Carl would snap to a halt, take in deep breaths of air, squint his eyes, and with strained ears, he would listen: Something...wandering outside his cave. He could feel it. Seconds would feel like hours as his bony, hardened body froze with acute accuracy…waiting. He was anxious, not afraid, simply curious about who or what might have come for a visit. It was Carl's hope to invite in a wandering beast with which to share a meal or a warm fire. But, as usual, nothing ever presented itself. With a final "sniff" he would retreat back inside and carry on like a kid with no rules.

      Sometimes Carl would shiver as an icy, mountain breeze would flutter the hairs on his body. His heart would race with excitement as he embraced the unapologetic, crisp chill of nature. When he was hot, he was glad his body was communing with the prickle of the sun. This only made Carl all the more happy to be a caveman because it meant that he was a *feeling* being. There was nothing else he would rather be than a partner, a piece that belonged, a family member among the scent of cedar trees, the tickle of grassy knolls, and the warmth of natural mineral springs. At night, he would be lulled to sleep, hypnotized by a symphony of coos, croaks, and clicks as his fellow creatures ushered in the dark skies. Carl was free.

****

Naked as a jaybird, I frolicked down the shore of the Oregon coast shouting at the top of my lungs, "I'm free! I'm free!" I was three and freed from my shorts. Somehow I had wrestled away from my mother's grip as she tried to put a bathing suit on me. All I needed was an opening- one narrow crack in the system. As fortune, or destiny, would have it, a space appeared where my mother needed to release her grip to put down the shorts and grab the suit. Free. In a split-second I was off. My mother ran after me half scolding me and half laughing at the sight. I was eventually caught, and the suit was firmly attached. Sunk, I resolved to dig.

      I've always wanted to be free, always. I wonder if this desire has been the fruition of some organic seed planted way back at the dawn of man-back in the caveman days. It would be easy to think of Adam as a caveman, you know, as his home was in a garden. A cave might have been quite a suitable place for him and Eve. I think Adam and Eve probably loved being naked and free in their cave. They might not have realized how much they loved it until they lost it though. I can picture a three-year-old Cain pulling the same stunt I did and his mother saying, "Now Cain, come on, put your animal skins back on...you can't be runnin' around naked all the time!" Centuries later, little Jeffy tries the same thing and gets the same response.

Since that day, I unknowingly began hiding myself behind myriads of masks. I've created psychological costumes that hide organic emotion. It's no wonder why I feel so constricted all the time. I've learned to play games, compensate, compromise, live by excuses (good ones, the ones that I don't think qualify as excuses), judge others and their game playing, and ultimately I find myself frustrated, misunderstood, tired and constipated-all because of clothes.

Turning 40 has caused me to do a little reflection. I'm trying to figure out where I lost being that piece that belonged. At what point did I allow a reinventing of myself? And so, I write as an attempt to get back to my origins. My hope is that as I reflect on my mistakes, knots, compromises, and disillusionments, maybe I'll find out where I got lost. I'm hoping Carl will find me and invite me back to the fire in the cave where I can start over, leave my costumes behind, and become naked and free again.

The Origins of Fear

Carl woke up in a cheerful mood as always. Stomach growling, he set off to fill his tummy with something delicious. As every other normal day, Carl went to a small tree hoping to eat its fruit. Now the trees were at the core of Carl's security. He counted on them. He didn't know how it worked, but he was very happy that they produced food for him all the time. He thought the trees must have felt as happy as he did to produce such wonderfully tasting fruit. It didn't make sense to Carl for an angry tree to be able to generate good fruit. He reasoned, therefore, that the tree must be a happy tree as the fruit was sweet.

As he walked beside a trickling creek on his way to the trees, he thought of how happy he was when he produced things. He thought of his cave drawings (which were quite good), the irrigation system he had built to bring water from the leaves into the half-shell of a coconut for his drinking enjoyment, the mud-baked tinder-box he made that housed his flint and coconut husk threads, and many other ingenious inventions created from his brilliant mind. These creations happened all the time because Carl was happy all the time. Something worked about it all, and this made him have faith in a lot of things.

As Carl rounded the final bend, just before he reached the glorious tree, his mouth started watering. But as quickly as it began, it went dry. Carl froze. He saw something...some*one*. There, in full-view, another caveman was eating from the fruit tree. A few feelings came over Carl that he had never felt before. At first, he felt excited to see another caveman who was doing the same things he would do. He could relate to this other caveman, and it made him feel welcomed. Carl knew that eating felt good and since *he* liked doing it, he imagined that the other caveman liked doing it too. Then, he felt conflicted. Carl was hungry, yet his fruit was being eaten by someone else. He didn't know how to explain it, but something began stirring in his chest. Carl bounded over to the other man. As Carl came closer, the other caveman jerked to a halt and stared. He examined Carl and tried to identify him. Carl approached the tree and grunted. The other mimicked the same grunt. They both were steady. The two looked at each other for a moment and then looked at the tree; there was one piece of fruit left. Both reached out at the same time to grab it. Both took hold of part of it. Carl tugged the fruit toward him. The other caveman yanked back. *Wham!* The two of them hit the ground struggling for possession. There was biting, clawing, and punching. Carl screamed as the other man sank his teeth into Carl's hand. Carl rolled up his fist and struck his opponent in the nose. Hair was pulled out, eyes were stabbed, bones were cracked. After a full fifteen minutes, the battle was over. Both of them were exhausted and bleeding. Having fought near the tree, they had accidentally broken its branches and uprooted it out of the wet soil.

The fruit, once plump and sweet, lay smashed at their feet. With nothing left to possess, and badly wounded from each other, they parted ways.

Once back at his cave, Carl tucked into a corner. He couldn't believe what had happened. He was jittery, shaking, and sore. A new feeling swept over him. He realized that if this other caveman was eating and enjoying the same food that he had, **maybe there wouldn't be enough for Carl when he became hungry again**. This changed everything. Carl freaked out and started to panic. This was a very foreign feeling as it made Carl feel extremely anxious, weak, and strong all at the same time. It was *fear*. "What if there isn't enough for me?" kept running through his mind as he rehearsed the scene of the other caveman taking and eating the fruit that he liked. Carl thought that if he saw this other caveman again he might throw a rock at him, but then he imagined missing, and the other caveman throwing it back and not missing. Considering that possibility, Carl relinquished the thought. Next, he thought he might go make some scary noises in the bushes, hoping that the other caveman would get scared and run away. But then he thought it could be embarrassing if the other caveman didn't run away and found him there snorting and wheezing in the bushes. Carl didn't know what to do. All he could think about was "What if there isn't enough left for me?"

Carl now felt a desperate focus to ensure his own survival. He had never thought about where food came from or how much food there actually was before. Now, however, Carl's mind was occupied with the possible fear of his extinction. His fear caused him to devote his thinking to a singular purpose- keeping himself alive.

His cave, which he normally associated

with a warm, welcoming spirit, had now become a fortress. He had to choose how he was going to live his life now that he had experienced incredible pain, frustration, and sorrow. This was the first time Carl made a choice driven by fear.

At first, he thought he would block the entrance to his cave so that no one could get in. But as he placed a few boulders in front of it, the light was prevented from coming in, and the cave became too cold. Removing the boulders made him feel better. He squatted and thought. A new idea came to him. He dashed out and retrieved a large branch, chiseled off some of the protrusions, and fashioned a weapon. This seemed to make more sense. He was protected. The club he had made gave him a sense of confidence and strength. However, the powerful feelings began to fade as he realized that it did nothing to take away the pain or his fear of starvation. Carl had hoped it would restore his happiness, but it didn't. Looking at the reformed branch, he thought of his beloved tree. His eyes flooded and he couldn't see. He put the club down and sobbed.

****

I cause problems. I am not comfortable

being human anymore. I could say that I have lost touch with my organic nature, my inner caveman if you will. Because of this, I've learned to negotiate my human-ness and what it means to be human. Instead of understanding my function and purpose of my human being-ness, I've traded my identity to play a game with the rest of humanity. It is worth noting (as far as I can tell) that humans are the only creatures who play this game. The animals, insects, frogs, etc. seem to do fine without laws, contracts, rules, games etc. They understand the natural order of things and live by an intrinsic law. They aren't troublemakers.

Do frogs wish they could be lions? I don't know, but it doesn't appear that they are trying to work at becoming lions. Frogs just keep being frogs. They do their thing everyday and though we don't see them all the time, we know that if we had to find one, we would have a pretty good idea where to go.

Now, I'm a different story. Somewhere along the line I decided to join in on a people game. This game has rules, laws, and contracts. Here are some of them:

1. Gather as much of everything as you can. When you see others gathering more than you, play the Fear card and draw two cards

from the "What if there isn't enough for me?" pile.

2. Always compare yourself to other humans to see if you are ok; if you don't measure up, play the Envy card or Self-Pity card, depending on which one will get you closer to winning.

3. If you draw the Honesty card, try to manipulate another player into buying it from you. If you are left with this card in your hand at the end of the game, you automatically lose. Playing the Honesty card will make people skeptical of you, and you will have to skip a turn.

4. If you are lucky enough to draw the Guilt card, use it on any players you'd like; it will help you take control of their assets. This can be very beneficial when you feel afraid and are in desperate need of staying in the game. (**Note: Be warned: If you play the Fear or Envy cards too many times, you limit your chances of drawing the Guilt card, and other players gain increased chances of drawing the Guilt card to use against you.)

5. Status points are given when players gain control over other players, have built impenetrable walls, are fluent in the language of the game, and have successfully avoided

implicitly trusting any other players. The player who gains the most Status points by the end of the game wins.

Because I joined this game, I now cause problems. When I am successful in the game, I'll see that I have thrown others under the bus to promote myself. To avoid being controlled by the Guilt card, I don't look back; I just keep striving for Status points. In all of this I find the game strangely unsatisfying. Something deep inside me tells me that I'm not supposed to be playing this game. My design is to be human, and this game takes away my humanity. Like a frog trying to become a lion,

I feel I am abandoning the beauty of what a human being is and does. I slowly become something that I am not. And when I try to unearth the reason I play this game, I find that fear is at the root… "What if there isn't enough for me?"

****

Carl had been fundamentally changed. Something felt different; his decisions were becoming more deliberate and less instinctive. He sat near the crackling fire he had made and thought. Where he used to think of beauty, he found that his thoughts were now of himself, his protection, his longevity. Ideas of peace and beauty had now been replaced with thoughts of pain, fear, and ultimately of non-existence. The mountain air that caressed his nostrils each morning became a clock instead of an exhilarating experience. These small changes in Carl's perspective produced new objectives for how he spent his day. He had things *to do* now. His survival depended on it. This fear caused him to question his right to belong.

    For an entire day, Carl sat in the center of his clammy cave. His muscles ached and pinched, shouting at him to use them, but he did not move. Carl's mind was creating a new kingdom driven by the power of fear. Though his joints, bones, and muscles responded negatively to the new control over his mind, Carl felt a sense of power in thinking this way. He felt…in charge. He began to play games with himself, testing how long he could endure the aches and pains of non-movement by the sheer will of his mind to do so. He began to realize something very powerful: *choice*. He could eat or refuse to eat. He could sleep or force himself to stay awake all night. Carl felt adrenaline rush through his veins, yet at the same time, he felt vulnerable and controlled. What used to feel naturally ordered and simple was now turning self-focused, myopic, and confusing. Carl felt trapped.

****

I've learned that fear about *"what ifs"* can determine all of one's decisions. People with phobias take extreme measures to make themselves feel safe. For example, there are people who have to check the locks on their doors several times to be sure that they locked them the first time. Even though they know they had locked them, a thought of *"what if* I didn't?" creeps in from somewhere and it eats away at them until they have to get up and go check again. The same goes for those with eating disorders who think, "*what if* I am too fat?" even though their reflections show severely underweight bodies. There are many "*what if*" scenarios out there that affect people: *What if* burglars might get me? *What if* I'm not smart enough? *What if* I don't have enough money? *What if* my kids end up hating me? *What if* I end up going to hell? *What if* I'm not perfect enough? *What if* I'm not pretty enough? *What if* I look under the rug, and what I think is there, IS actually there? *What if* I'm not as sick as I want to believe that I am? *What if* I fail? The power behind "*what ifs*" is *doubt*. If you really want to mess people up, throw a little doubt on them. This method has worked since the beginning, just ask the serpent in the Garden of Eden story. Everything was going fine until the snake threw in the little "zinger" and said, "Did God really say not to eat of the fruit?" Doubt makes an otherwise completely sensible thought turn to mush in an instant. It lets the exception to the rule become the rule. But doubt is fueled by something even more powerful…*pain*. Whether actual pain or the mere belief in potential pain, both can fundamentally influence the decision-making process. So, the fear thing goes like this:

Once upon a time, a man, listening to his organic instincts, realized he was hungry and decided to get some lunch...

I like avoiding pain, and fear is a good mechanism for that. It keeps me out of risky situations and makes me feel kind of safe in a way. Ironically, fear makes me feel caged too. It's like being inside a bubble. By trapping me inside, it can keep potential pain away. I lose out on life, but I don't have to experience pain.

Fear has caused me to do a lot of stupid things. When I'm afraid, I naturally begin to think only of my own protection. I'm not really talking about the "frightened" type of afraid. What I'm talking about is that my identity and placement in the eyes of others feels threatened and insecure. Aren't arguments based on this very thing? One person feels the intense need to be validated and understood, while the other person is feeling the exact same way? Insecurity peaks because one person is afraid that the other will disregard his or her feelings on the matter. Fear is the defense mechanism that is utilized by our psyche to avoid the pain that is crouching at the door. It acts kind of like our nerves do. For example, when we get cut, our nerves let our brain know that we feel pain. Once we feel pain, we can look at the cut and stop the bleeding so we won't bleed to death. If we didn't feel pain, we would be bleeding all over the place, not living very long lives. Fear functions the same way. If we didn't feel threatened or afraid, we might run into a lot of pain. But, what I need to determine is whether pain is *really* crouching at the door as often as I think. It may be the case that I have just learned how to safeguard myself from potential pain by allowing myself to *feel* threatened. Naturally, my reaction is to threaten others in order to protect myself. It seems to me that it's a big game of deceit based on the power of suggestion.

****

Carl had trouble sleeping that night. The noises he heard outside of his cave that once put him to sleep sounded...different. Every few minutes, he would slither over to the cave entrance and peer outside, thinking he heard his enemy creeping up on him. When he didn't see anything unusual, he would tiptoe back to his dank corner. Carl was irritated. He became bothered by the weather when it was too cold or too hot. He was often easily frustrated and began sighing and mumbling a lot. He started to do something new-*complain*. He now noticed that his cave seemed too cramped and he thought it smelled funny. Then, when it took him three minutes instead of two to start a fire, he threw his flint out the cave door. The complaining gave him a way to get his fear out-the fear that the other caveman might actually be eating all of the food and that Carl might be slowly dying. But complaining was like a pestering itch. When scratched, it felt better for a minute, but it quickly began itching again until it was scratched some more-kind of like a mosquito bite. As a result, Carl became frustrated pretty much all the time. He complained about the hot sun, the wet rain, his damp cave, his sore body, the gross smells in the air, the annoying sounds outside, how hungry he was, and all kinds of other things. No longer did Carl's thoughts align with his organic instincts. Each thought became a wrestling match between what he felt was natural to do and what he felt he had to do.

****

Can you remember the last time you made a decision based on what felt like the most organic and natural thing to do? I think most of my decisions don't include this consideration. Most of my decisions are based on rubrics like, "Will this give me the competitive edge?" and "Will others affirm this decision?" Following your organic instinct takes guts. There is risk involved. I haunt myself with thoughts of "What if I choose to really go after something that makes sense to me (for reasons no one understands but my mind and me) and I fail? If I fail, my friends and family members will surely ridicule me." Because of these fears, I often choose to stay put, and do nothing. It's safer. I won't have to answer any questions, I won't have to apologize, I won't have to admit that I've miscalculated. The irony is that on the flip side, had I taken a big risk, endured the questioning, tolerated the "nay-sayers", and actually pulled it off, then they'd all gather around bragging about how we are friends and relatives. Since it takes many failures to eventually succeed, most of the time I choose to stay put and talk myself into being satisfied with a wish.

****

Without any contest, my favorite books as a kid were the *Choose Your Own Adventure* books. While my brother was reading novels, I wanted to play outside and discover things. I would beg my mom to make him play with me. She would often make him put down his book, which he hated, and force him on an outdoor adventure with me. However, there were times when, to be fair, I was the one who had to give in and had to "read" instead. So, reading a *Choose Your Own Adventure* book was like playing outside for me: free form… my decisions…my adventure. What was special about these books was that at the bottom of most pages, the reader would get to choose the direction the story went. Each scene ended with a decision to make. The decision the reader made led to different pages in the book. If one chose wisely, the story kept continuing. If one made a foolish choice, the story would end in some crazy turn of unfortunate events.

It was a great series because it taught me how to live vicariously through the characters and how to accept the fate of my own decisions. If I died because a ten-headed spider was living in the cave that I thought would be interesting to explore, I learned that I needed to be cautious before making rash decisions. On the other hand, I was rewarded with more chances to steer the story the way I wanted to if I took reasonable risks. Sometimes, even when I thought I had made a reasonable decision, it didn't always work, and

I ended up shipwrecked on a deserted island. The idea that I was in charge of my fate made the stories so much fun to experience. On the whole, these books taught me a lot about life. They taught me about risk and reward, the consequences of impulsivity, and how to live with, or repair, poor decisions. They helped me build confidence, which in turn, deflated any fear.

Since then, I have encountered many crossroads and many ugly spiders staring me down. I have had to make several decisions where life-changing consequences have hung in the balance. Some decisions, made with foolish motivations, turned out to cause more pain and suffering. Others, made with wise motivations (though also causing emotional disturbances at first), delivered a renewed sense of peace, confidence, and purpose. I'm not sure how to tell in advance which decisions are the life-changing ones. Crossroads just seem to appear from time to time, and decisions must be made. Often, the funny part is that I may be standing at the crossroads for months before figuring out that a choice is set before me. Once realized, however, there is no getting around it; I must choose. It usually happens like this:

I've been digging a proverbial hole for a very long time. The light is slowly fading as I get deeper and deeper, motivated by god knows what. I'm seeking for something I think will satisfy the impulse of my digging. Maybe I think I know what it is, maybe I don't. Regardless, I dig. Then, one day, when all the planets line up, I look up and see that I'm in a big hole. I peer down and see that I haven't found what I am digging for. I stare straight ahead at the moist earth in front of me and enter a daze. In this daze I realize I have a decision to make: Do I keep digging because I might find what I'm looking for in just a few *more shovel fulls? If so, turn to life page 47. Do I stop digging because I've been a jerk, and I need to resolve to work myself out of the pointless hole I've dug? If so, turn to life page 33.*

****

One night, as Carl was battling festering thoughts of fear and anger, a sinister notion seized Carl's mind; he imagined the other caveman gathering up all of the food in the entire land. The hair on Carl's back stood on end. He imagined the man mocking him, laughing, and eating to his heart's desire while Carl starved to death. Carl let out a wicked scream that echoed against the walls of his cave. A flock of birds fluttered frantically out of some nearby bushes at the sound. This was the last straw. Carl galloped out of his cave full of anger and desperation; he was determined to stop his enemy. He charged through the underbrush brandishing his arms, breaking branches, destroying small homes of several critters, smashing flowers under his broad, miscalculated strides until he rounded upon the trunk of the fallen fruit tree. Looking down at it, Carl's eyebrows furrowed. His eyes narrowed, his nostrils flared, and with clenched jaws and gritted teeth, he released his fear-filled anger and kicked the tree as hard as he could. The pain Carl felt was unbelievable. Jolts of lightning shot up his legs as blood gushed from the end of his toes. Four of his five toes were crushed, protruding at unnatural angles. His heart, stomach, and mind all felt faint at the same time. He curled up in a ball hugging his hairy foot close to him, rocking back and forth violently, as he spewed out a mix of guttural screams and unintelligible words. Carl was completely raw. Hobbling over to the nearby stream, he thrust his mangled toes into the cool, running water. Liquid healing rushed over his bloody sinews, and with clinched eyes, Carl winced and howled. Making the sound of an enormous siren, Carl's mouth flashed between what looked like a small, pursed "O" and an enormous forced smile as he grew faint with pain.

Realization finally set in. Carl lifted his eyes, stared, and entered a daze. He thought about the origin of his fear. He had reached a defining moment, and at this point in the story, so have you. A choice must be made. What will happen next? Will he rise up and use the power of pain and fear to unleash the full extent of his rage upon his enemy? Or, will the severe physical and emotional pain jar him into a sense of "this isn't working." Let your mind trail down these two paths. Both stories hold valuable lessons. Choose your own adventure.

www.ingramcontent.com/pod-product-compliance
Lightning Source LLC
Chambersburg PA
CBHW032113040426
42337CB00040B/548